45 Essential Skills To Survive Natural Disaster In Your Own Home And In The Wilderness

Table of content:

Survival Guide

TOP 20 IDEAS

HOW TO SURVIVE NATURAL DISASTER IN YOUR HOME

Survival Guide:

TOP 20 Ideas How to Survive Natural Disaster in Your Home

Introduction: You Better Be Prepared

You have to be prepared in life, and there can be no doubt that this world gives us plenty to prep for. From brutally hot summers to ice cold winters, Mother Nature seems to be working overtime with the disasters she routinely dishes out. But if you follow the step by step instructions presented here in this book, you won't have anything to worry about. Every step of your survival is presented in perfect clarity no matter what sort of natural disaster may come your way. So, buckle up your seat belts folks, and get prepared for the ride! Because when it comes to the dangers of Mother Nature and the natural disasters she often provides, this little book is your perfect guide!

Chapter 1: Every Prepper's Nightmare—What to Avoid

You picked up this book to hear what it is you should do during a natural disaster, but just as important as knowing what to do, is knowing what *not to do*. Here in this chapter we will highlight some of the biggest mistakes, bungles, mishaps, and misnomers that people make when it comes to prepping for natural disasters. Here is what you should avoid.

Avoid Panic

The last thing that you want to do during any crisis situation is panic. If you panic you lose your focus, and if you lose your focus you could lose your life. In order to have a fixed level of concentration you need to give yourself a case of tunnel vision. Try focusing on one thing at a time, instead of scattershot distractions. Let's take for example, a sudden power outage in the middle of the night. How exactly should you handle it?

Well—instead of panicking, jumping up, bumping into the wall, and tripping and falling on your face, take a deep breath, use your cellphone as a flashlight, and make your way to the kitchen drawer where you store your candles and matches (or wherever it is that you store such things), and focus on lighting them. With this one step taken care of, you can then focus on the next. In order to avoid panic, and not be overwhelmed, strategically move from task to task until you succeed.

<u>*Don't Ignore the Authorities*</u>

In the middle of an emergency, don't be tempted to go it on your own and blatantly ignore warnings and directions from civil authorities. There are many cases of folks blatantly disregarding orders to evacuate in the face of an emergency who have failed to survive as a result. It is called the "Emergency Broadcast System" for a reason—it is meant to be broadcast as an emergency message in a time of crisis. Whatever you do, don't ignore the authorities who are in charge of your safety.

<u>*Planning at the Very Last Minute*</u>

A natural disaster should not be put off until the last minute, there are several things that you should do to prepare for the event. You should have adequate supplies at least a week ahead of time, and you should have a safehouse prepared if need be, in advance. Your home should be fortified and structurally prepped well ahead of time. Instead of planning at the last minute, make sure all of your bases are covered early on in the game.

Packing Unnecessary Things

The last thing you should do during an emergency is bog yourself down with extra baggage. If you don't need something for survival, then don't bring it. You should never waste precious time, space, and energy worrying over trivial pursuits, and instead focus on the main goal of the endeavor. All you need to pack are the necessities. Make sure you bring some food, water, and perhaps an extra pair of socks and underwear at most. Don't try to pack your whole wardrobe for an emergency evacuation from natural disaster.

Not Letting Anyone Know Where You Are

This is a major mistake that many novices make. They think they have everything under control and they don't have to tell anyone where they are or what they are doing during a disaster. But if the home you are in becomes so flooded that you have to get up on top of the roof and flag down a helicopter, it would certainly have helped if you had let others know where you were to begin with! Be sure to avoid all of these detrimental habits and behaviors as you prep for the next natural disaster.

Chapter 2: How to Survive Hurricanes, Tornadoes, and Flash Floods

From Hurricane Harvey to the tornadoes and floods that have devastated the Mid-Western United Sates, Mother Nature has dealt mankind some rather punishing blows as of late. There can be no doubt that this excessive and extreme weather has really taken its toll. But there are steps you can take to mitigate the damage and duress as much as possible. Here in this chapter we will explore your options in the face of the storm.

Have a Hurricane Evacuation Plan

The very first thing that anyone should do in the face of an oncoming hurricane is prepare an evacuation plan. You should make certain that you know the best evacuation route, and safest passage away from the danger zone. This means you should be aware of things such as elevation levels, and high-water mark regions, so that you can avoid them, and choose the quickest most secure roadways to safety. Have a go-bag to stash vital supplies in ready just in case you do have to evacuate at the last minute, and make sure that your car is full of gas. Because sometimes just being able to make a break for it is the best survival plan you could ever have.

Find a Hurricane/Tornado Safe Room

Both hurricanes and tornadoes have the potential of ripping the roof right off your house, and sending all manner of debris hurtling your way. But if you are unable to flee from an oncoming storm, you need to make sure you can go to the safest part of your home to ride it out. This usually means selecting a centralized location in the home that can then be further fortified against wind and debris. The safe room of the home is basically an improvised version of a storm shelter.

The safest place would typically be close to the middle of the structure. Bathrooms are also a fairly safe place to be, since they are typically well insulated from windows and other potentially dangerous objects. Preferably safe rooms should also be equipped with inward opening doors. This is to prevent you from getting trapped inside after the storm subsides. Because there have been many cases of folks safely riding out a storm in their safe room only to find their exit blocked by fallen debris after the storm is over.

You see, it doesn't take much for a hurricane or tornado to pin your bedroom dresser on top of your door. And if your door only opens by pushing it outward, it would be essentially blocked and locked in place by this obstruction. But if your door opens inward, rather than outward, you could still open the door and then work to push the debris out of the way. Keep all of these things in mind when prepping your hurricane and tornado safe room.

In a specific localized area, tornadoes can be just as deadly as hurricanes. And if you live in a home that is not structurally strong such as a trailer or apartment. You need to get out of them if you can. If not however, you need to hunker down and make the best of it. Just like in the above mentioned safe room, you need to find a place you can go where there are no windows, or loose and potentially hazardous debris. Once you are in this safety zone, you need to literally put your head down. If you ever did a "duck and cover" drill in school, you should know the routine.

And as the tornado hits, you need to duck down and cover your head. To further ensure your survival it wouldn't be a bad idea to get under a strong table or desk, this structure could serve as a barrier and shield to protect you from falling and flying debris.

And if you happen to be out on the road when the storm hits, you need to find shelter immediately. Do not try to outrace the storm, because unlike what you may have seen in the movies, cars are just not equipped to drive that fast!

On average, tornadoes travel at speeds in excess of 100 miles an hour! And even if you think your souped-up hotrod can go from zero to 120 miles an hour, it doesn't matter.

Because you have to realize, that unlike you, the tornado doesn't have to travel along the roadways, it is free to go in any and every direction. And while you are sitting in your car watching a twister right in front of you, it could change course and head your way in an instant.

By the time you struggle to put your car in reverse to turn around, it will be too late. If you want to survive a tornado, you are going to want to stay off the roads. And if you do find yourself driving when a tornado hits, and unable to get to shelter immediately, the best thing for you to do is to get out of the car and head for a ditch. Getting down low to the ground inside a ditch is probably the best protection you could find in such a situation, so don't hesitate to do it.

Surviving Flash Floods

Finding yourself suddenly at the mercy of a flash flood is no easy thing to deal with. They are called "flash" floods for a reason, because these guys are as fast as a flash! Just picture it. You are driving down the road in a rain storm and the next thing you know you have water up to your driver's side window. That is just how rapidly things can deteriorate when you are dealing with flash floods. If you are inside your vehicle and find yourself subjected to a natural disaster like this, you need to immediately turn around and drive for higher ground.

And if you are unable to drive to safety—then by all means—get out of the car and make a run for it on foot! Remember, your life is more important than your car! You can always get another vehicle but you can't get another life! Be advised that in some circumstances with rapidly rising water you may not be able to get your door open in time. This is due to water pressure on the door. If you find this to be the case, the best thing to do is just bust open your window. An easy way to do this, is to grab hole of your metal seat belt buckle and smash it right into the glass.

At any rate, you need to break the window, and climb out as soon as possible. If you are walking out on foot and notice that the water level is rising, stay away from any naturally occurring bodies of water. If you are near a river, move away from the river edge, near a lake walk in the other direction, and so on and so forth. Also, if you are in a wilderness environment and happen to notice high water marks on trees and other landmarks—even if it is not flooded at the moment—this is a clear indication that this is an area that is particularly vulnerable to flash floods, and should be avoided if heavy rain begins to descend. This is how you can survive a flash flood.

Chapter 3: How to Survive the Worst of the Winter

Recent winter weather has been particularly harsh. And even while the debate rages on over climate change and global warming, many of us in the Northern Hemisphere find ourselves routinely snowed in from December to February. We often hear phrases and terms such as "arctic blast" and "polar vortexes". But all we really know as that bone cold air hits us right in the face, as we shovel and scrape our way out of the blizzard, is that the extremes of winter weather have just made our lives that much more difficult. This chapter provides you with the tip and tricks you need to dig yourself out of the worst of the winter.

Pack Some Warm Clothes

The last thing you want to do during horribly cold winter weather is go out underdressed or without warm clothing. The key to staying warm during the winter months is to wear layers. You should always wear an undershirt, an over shirt, a light sweater, coat, overcoat, and a warm pair of gloves. These layers will help shield you from the winter frost. You should also cover your head. They say that about half of all our body heat escapes right out of our heads every single day. So, cover your head with a warm winter hat to stay warm.

Prep a Fire Drill

Yes, my friends, this is indeed still a book on winter prep, and no, we are not speaking of the weekly "Fire Drills" you had in Middle School in which you had to line up and pretend your school was on fire. Nope, that is not what we are talking about here. The "fire drill" we speak of in this section is actually an ancient fire-starting tool of the Native Americans, in which a stick or finely carved piece of wood is rolled between the hands and "drilled" into a board of wood to spark a campfire.

Anyone who finds themselves stuck out in the cold tundra could make use of this simple but effective device. Now, for the sake of clarity, let me repeat one more time how this contraption is used. Basically, you just take a stick, approximately a foot or two long, and you stand it up on a thin wooden board. This board is actually referred to as a "fire board" but its essentially just a thin piece of wood. Situate your fire drill upright on the fireboard, and place the upper mid-section of the stick between your two outstretched, flat palms.

Vigorously roll the fire drill back and forth with the bottom of the stick quickly spinning against the surface of the fireboard. This action is what creates the friction that will spark a fire. Use this spark to set any tinder you have, such as twigs, leaves, charcoal, or whatever else you have, ablaze. Knowing how to prep a fire drill is a great skill to have, and a guaranteed way to stay warm in the cold.

Get a Blizzard Bag

If you get hit with the blizzard bug, then you should get yourself a blizzard bag. This means gathering together a bag of emergency supplies that you would use during a bad snow storm. In this blizzard bag you should have, a good snow shovel, ice scrapers, and any other tool that might be important when it comes to digging through wet and snowy weather. Along with these, you should also make sure to stash a conventional flashlight, batteries, a cell phone charger, and even a bag of cat litter. Yes—cat litter! Many people are not aware of it, but cat litter works wonders when it comes to cars stuck in the snow. Just put a little bit of cat litter underneath your stuck tires, give it a little gas and you are good to go!

Use Sun Absorbent Windows

Even under the best of circumstances, winter weather can get rather chilly, rather fast. But imagine just how bad things would get if your power were to go out, and you have no other means of heating. Your home and your body temperature would get dangerously cold in a relatively short period of time.

But even with no other recourse, all you have to do is look to that yellow ball of gas in the sky, and the sun to bail you out! Even in the coldest of winters, the sun still manages to shine down on us for at least a few hours every day.

If you could just capture some of those rays and use them for your advantage you could spare yourself much of the cold. The best way to do this is to turn your homes windows into mini solar sun absorbers. This is done by taking a piece of cardboard and cutting it into the shape of your windows. Now take some black spray paint and thoroughly coat the board with black paint. Black, is of course a sun absorbent material. Put this black cardboard up into your windows to absorb sunlight. These simple, yet incredibly useful, solar attracting boards, will now heat up your home in no time.

Apply Insulation and Weather Stripping

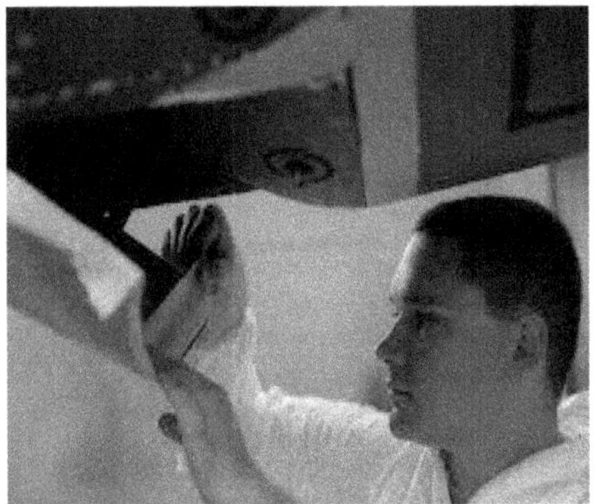

It can't be stressed enough how important good insulation and weather stripping really are. Most homes lose a lot of heat through cracks in their doors and windows, but if you were to just put some thin layers of weather stripping inside to fill those gaps, the heat of the home will be retained. The easiest way to pinpoint these gaps in doors and windows is to hold a lit flame, such as a match or cigarette lighter up to the frames of your doors and watch as drafts move the flame, these drafts will indicate the exact spots you need to install your weather stripping.

As for the insulation of your home, you should take care to make sure that draft prone areas such as your attic are adequately insulated. In order to avoid gusts of cold wind blowing into your home and warm air seeping out, make sure you put sufficient layers of insulation up in the rafters of the attic. As it turns out, your attic is the structural head of your house, and about half all your homes heat seeps out of it. So just like you need to put a warm hat on your own head during the winter months, you should put a warm hat on the roof of your home by insulating your attic.

Can and Store Plenty of Food, Store Excess Water

Canning has kept populations all over the globe well fed in even the worst of circumstances. And it is completely feasible for someone to store up as much as a year's worth of food through the process of simply canning them in pressurized jars. Canning can preserve the integrity of food almost indefinitely. All you have to do to can your own jars is find a typical "mason jar" and stuff it with your produce. Next, put a sealing lid on the jar, tighten it, and place the jar in the center of a pot full of boiling hot water. Allow it to boil and pressurize for several minutes, and your food for the winter is canned!

Even more important than food is having an adequate supply of drinkable water. Because believe me—in the middle of a winter storm you don't want to have to resort to drinking that funny looking yellow snow you found outside! So, in order to avoid this fate, be sure to pack several bottles of water before the snowy weather hits. In an emergency you can also tap into excess water from your water heater, and even water in your toilet tank! Hey—it may not always be pretty—but it's survival!

Chapter 4: Surviving Fire and Earthquakes

If you live on the West Coast of the United States, the two biggest threats that you face are out of control wild fires and unpredictable Earth tremors, all the way to devastating earthquakes. In this chapter we highlight some of the best ways to handle and manage these life-impacting natural disasters.

Fire Preparedness

The first step in ensuring your survival is always preparation. And this couldn't be truer than when it comes to fire safety. You need to have your smoke detectors checked frequently and you need to have a clear path to exit your home. The number one problem that many face when confronted with a fire is not having an adequate way out the door. Make sure that the hallway is clear of clutter and your doors free of debris, so that you can point yourself, and your loved ones in the right direction. As you can see, just being prepared is half the battle.

Surviving the Blaze

If you find yourself caught right in the middle of a fire, the first thing you need to do is get down as low to the ground as possible. The reason for this is quite simple. Heat rises. This means then, that during the course of a fire, the upper levels of the home will be much hotter than the lower levels. The level of heat could fluctuate to such an extent, that the ceiling of a home on fire, could be as hot as a roasting oven, while the floor remains just a few degrees above normal room temperature.

Also, the smoke of the fire will no doubt be the most prolific up in the rafters then down on the ground. So, get down on the floor and crawl to the exit. And if you can't get to an immediate exit door, you might have to make one. If you are near a picture window for example, you could take an object or even your bear hands to break it open. If you do get to a door however, before reaching for that doorknob, it would be wise to remember that this door knob may very well be red hot.

If it is, you can take off your shirt, or some other article of clothing and use it as a kind of protective glove—if you will—and with its protection from the heat, you can quickly fling the door open, and make your escape. As soon as you are out, position yourself far away from the flames as you wait for first responders to arrive. If you keep all of these tips and precautions in mind, you will be able to survive the blaze completely unscathed.

Healing Burns with Aloe Vera

If you have ever been burned you know just how horrible it feels. Our skin is our point of contact with the outside world, and when it is significantly damaged through a bad burn, even a sudden breeze against its surface could be excruciating. And as much as we can try to prepare for the calamity that a fire would represent, there is always the chance we could be caught off guard enough to suffer a burn injury.

If this is the case, you need to take immediate measures to make sure that the injury does not get worse. This means that you need to bandage the injured part of your body up and place ointment on its surface. One of the best ointments for this task is Aloe Vera. Aloe Vera gel scooped directly out of the Aloe Vera plant is soothing and healing. Just place it right on the skin and wrap the injured area up, and you will be on the road to recovery in no time.

Predicting the Big Quake

The vast majority of us, are probably under the assumption that earthquakes are a far away problem, that would never affect us. If you live in North America for example, you no doubt associate a quake with the West Coast. But despite what you may think, there are many more places other than California and Oregon that are subjected to quakes. The truth is, an earthquake can happen anywhere. The only reason that we are led to believe that earthquakes only happen in certain locations is because of how earthquakes are forecast.

You see, while there is no doppler radar that can spot big quakes, several days ahead of time, quakes are predicted by statistics and past precedent. But in the end, this form of statistical reasoning is not an exact science, and merely a hypothetical guess at best. In reality, earthquakes can occur anywhere, at any time. In fact, the biggest earthquake on record is not on the West Coast at all—it occurred right in the middle of the nation in Missouri. Yes, Missouri.

In 1811 an earthquake hit the state of Missouri that was said to be so powerful, that it caused rooftop chimneys to collapse as far away as Cincinnati, Ohio! So, having that said, we cannot always rely on statistical averages when it comes to predicting the next big quake. The truth of the matter is, an earthquake can happen anytime, anywhere, so no matter where we are located, we must be prepared.

<u>*Dealing with the Aftermath of an Earthquake*</u>

During an earthquake there are several things that you should consider. You should make sure that you have a safe place to ride out the quake away from falling debris, this is rather obvious. But what people often forget is how to deal with the aftermath. In order to prevent hazardous conditions in your home after a quake, you need to turn off the electric, water and gas utilities.

Because in the aftermath of a quake, all of these could pose a potential hazard. Ruptured pipes can flood the home, gas lines could burst and create an explosive hazard, and ripped electrical lines can lead to electrocution. In the aftermath of the quake, make sure that all of these things are taken care of, and accounted for.

Conclusion: Home Grown Survival

The world is full of danger, and crisis can strike us at a moment's notice. But even though natural disasters are on the rise, that doesn't mean that we can't prepare for it. And if you take the 20 proven survival strategies presented in this book to heart, regardless of the occasion or the natural disaster—wind, rain, sleet, earthquake, or snow—you will be able to make it through. Because home is where the heart is, and when it comes to natural disasters and all the other threats we face, a little home-grown survival could do us all a whole lot of good.

Lewis Forman
BAREBONES
Outdoor Survival:
25 DIY Essential Hacks to Survive
In The Wilderness And Stay Alive

Outdoor Survival:

25 DIY Essential Hacks to Survive in The Wilderness and Stay Alive

Introduction: The Great Outdoors

The world outside of your door, is as beautiful as it is perilous. There are many unknown dangers that you may face, this book seeks to ameliorate these troubles with 25 hacks to help you survive any contingency you may face in the wilderness.

In the world of today, it seems that the very second that we step outside of our familiar surroundings we become lost. When we step away from our finely manicured cities and out into the great outdoors we have no idea how to proceed. Everything is so foreign to us, we might as well be on another planet.

This is why it is so important to reacquaint yourself with the natural environment. Get yourself familiar once again with the sights, sounds, and smells of the natural world. If it helps—lets exercise our imagination, and think about our trek through the wild before we even begin.

Imagine that you are at the foot of a mountain, looking over a group of wooded trees. As you stare into the woods you take in the color scheme of the foliage. You can see dark browns, slowly converging with light greens, and everything perfectly finding its place in this natural landscape.

Now picture yourself stepping into the forest, and taking your first strides across the forest floor, crunching tree branches and other debris as you travel. Look around at what your walking on, plant and animal life, some of it living, others long decayed. You see berries growing in trees and even from the dead matter on tree trunks as you find mushrooms sprouting up, gaining nourishment from the dead tree. As you can see, everything in this environment is working together in cohesion in a perfect system of life and death.

As you too go into the great outdoors, just think of yourself as another piece of this vibrant patchwork. In order to allow yourself a fruitful sojourn into the wilderness you will have to tune yourself into this framework, and keep yourself aware of the ecosystem of which you are actively apart. Awaken yourself to the possibilities as you step out of your old comfort zone, and into the great outdoors.

Chapter 1: Learn to use Navigation

By and large, the biggest challenge most face with the wilderness is simply not getting lost. We are all used to signs and guide posts telling us where to turn and which way to go. And if there isn't a sign, we can usually simply pull out our phone and use GPS to guide us to where we need to be. But what if we can't always depend on modern technology to guide us? Are there other ways to navigate through the wilderness? You bet there are! And this chapter highlights the best of them!

The Compass

At its most basic level, a compass is simply a closed off container, with a floating, magnetized needle inside of it. This needle doesn't even point to "True North", but instead points to "Magnetic North". This means that on a compass, the north that the needle points to isn't the North Pole on top of the planet, but rather, the northernmost focal point of the planet's magnetic field. Rather than being situated on the North Pole of the planet, Magnetic North is actually situated over Ellesmere Island in Northern Canada!

As a consequence, all magnetic compasses are in reality pointing to this same Canadian island, which is about 1000 miles away from the North Pole!

But even though compasses point to Magnetic North rather than True North, they are still pointing in a northerly direction, and as long as you aren't planning on trekking further north than Ellesmere, a magnetic needle should be able to take you where you need to go. The compass's unrelenting magnetic needle, which points to the same location no matter where you go, will keep you from going in circles, and help to chart a clear path through the wilderness.

And if you don't want to buy a compass, you can easily make your own. All you really need to do, is take a regular sewing needle and vigorously rub it with a piece of cloth. Do this long enough and you will develop a static, magnetic charge. Once the needle has been charged up like this, place it in a cup of water. The needle will now invariably point to Magnetic North. It's a crude survival trick, but in a real pinch, it will at least help you get your bearings.

Navigating with Binoculars

The common pair of binoculars are a tried and true standard of survival navigation. The weakest pair of binoculars you might find, is still able to magnifying human vision ten times greater than it normally is. Binoculars work by focusing light down into the binocular lens and back toward the retinas of the user, creating the perceived magnification of sight. If your navigation through the wilderness ever encounters any difficulty, just put on a pair of binoculars and you will be able see far enough through the trees to find your way back once again.

Binoculars are a great tool to cut through the fog of confusion. I can remember a time that me and a fellow hiker were lost for nearly an hour, walking around in circles, unable to find our camp. My friend then suddenly reminded me that I was carrying a pair of binoculars in my coat pocket. I took those binoculars out and stared out of them to scan the horizon. And sure, enough I spotted the smoke from our still glowing campfire. It was thanks to those binoculars that we were able to find our way back. Be sure to pack some of your own.

Read a Topographical Map

Topographical maps serve as literal representations of geological features on the ground. Such maps are necessary in the wilderness where there are no roads, and signs to use as points of reference. Instead these maps rely upon real features in the local environment such as lakes, rivers, mountains, and forests. These maps rely upon a color-coded key in order to convey to the user, just what they are looking at. Some are rather obvious, such as green being an indication of trees and grass, and blue representing bodies of water.

But there are also regions of white that tell us of an open expanse, and shades of brown which indicate mountains, and hills. Contour lines are also a common feature that serves to indicate the level of elevated ground in the region. If you are planning on outdoor survival, you will want one of these maps. You can usually find a topographical map at most National Park offices, and you can of course buy them online or at local brick and mortar distributors.

Chapter 2: Building Outdoor Shelters

Before you consider anything else about outdoor survival you should consider just how you are going to put a roof over your head. Because being exposed to the elements is not only inconvenient, it is downright dangerous. Torrential rains can pour down out of nowhere, leaving you soaked to the bone. This is just how easily unsheltered hikers can catch pneumonia and perish. To avoid such a fate for yourself, be sure to build an outdoor shelter.

Mud Shelter

Mud shelters are still used all over the world as wilderness dwellings, composed of nothing more than the mud and dirt in the immediate environment. The key to building these structures is to find soil that has a somewhat clay-like mixture, which will be malleable in your hands. But before you begin shaping your mud, you are going to need to lay out your foundation. Do this by taking a stick and tracing a large rectangle, about five feet wide, and ten feet long into the ground.

Now go and gather several sticks, all about 2 or 3 feet long. Take these sticks and place them all along the edges of this rectangle. With this stick foundation established, start mixing a little water with some nearby dirt.

Take this mud mixture and begin slathering it all over the stick foundation. Do this until the sticks are completely covered with mud. After this, you can begin building your mud bricks. Create bricks out of your dirt that are 6 inches long and 3 inches thick. Stack these up all along the mud/stick foundation. Build up walls that are at least 4 feet high.

Now go find some branches that are about 5 feet long, and begin laying them across the 5-foot space between the mud walls. Now gather up as much brush—things like sticks, twigs, leaves, and rocks and place them all over the branches to further insulate and cover the gaps. Finally, create a final batch of mud and slather it all over the branches and brush of your roof, until everything is perfectly sealed up tight. Your mud shelter is ready to give you refuge from the wilderness.

Lean-To Shelter

The "lean-to-shelter" is a classic emergency, wilderness home. All you need are some very simple commodities from the environment such as tree-bark, sticks, leaves, and rocks. These are the basic materials that will be used to fill the frame of your "lean to". The frame itself consists of two sturdy branches with another branch overlaying the top of them. Find two branches that are both about 3 feet long. Take these branches and plant them up in the ground, standing upright, about 2 feet apart from each other.

Now get a third branch and lay it on top of the two upright branches. You can make the process easier by cutting a groove into the tops of each of these branches so that you can lay the horizontal branch right across. Once the horizontal branch is in place, your basic lean-to frame is complete. Upon this frame you are going to place further sticks and branches, "leaning" them across the structure. Thereby completing this wilderness shelter. Its not the most robust of shelters, but it will keep the rain off your head.

Squirrel's Nest Shelter

Probably the most basic shelter of all, this wilderness structure consists of just a pile of debris strategically gathered together such as leaves, sticks, and twigs, and placed into one large mound. An individual can then duck down inside this leafy pile to hide or gain temporary shelter from the elements. One major drawback of such a shelter would be possible insects in the mound, and other questionable sanitary matters. But regardless, if you need to bury yourself in a hurry, the Squirrel's Nest Shelter will get the job done for you.

Native American's used Tipi structures for thousands of years as a wilderness refuge from the elements. They were quite useful for their hunter gatherer lifestyle due to their durability yet lightness in weight. These Tipi's could be easily picked up in a moment's notice and taken to new hunting grounds. This mobility is still a useful factor for any would-be survivalist today, since with a Tipi as a shelter you are not stuck in any one spot of the wilderness environment, since you can pick up your Tipi and take it with you wherever you may go. To create your own Tipi, requisition for yourself three 4-foot-long branches. Stand these branches up in a tripod formation, and tie the tops of the branches together. Now simply throw animal skin, blankets, or a tarp over the tripod frame and your Tipi is ready for business.

Yurt

Similar to the Tipp, these ancient structures, rely upon a circular wooden frame, with animal skin thrown over them. All you have to do is draw out a circle in the ground, and then place a series of 2 to 3-foot-tall sticks all around the circle. Ben the sticks toward the center, and tie the tops of the sticks together. This is your frame. Now just throw animal skin, blankets, or even tarp over the structure and your Yurt is ready to go. If it was good for Genghis Khan on the Mongolian Steppes, it can be good for you, in your own wilderness situation as well!

Chapter 3: Finding Clean Water

If you aren't well hydrated, you won't be able to think clearly. And if you go without water for long enough, you won't even be able to stay alive, let alone find your way back to camp. Most can only go a few days without water, and anything after that period, is a slow decline to death. This is why it is so crucial to not only find water while you are in the wilderness but also to know how to clean and purify your water so that it is suitable to drink. This chapter will discuss all of the methods and strategies available for you to do just that.

Boil Surface Water

The easiest way to get water in the wilderness just might be to simply scoop it up from the surface of nearby rivers, lakes, and streams. But you better beware, because even if this surface water looks to be in pristine condition, you never know what contamination and pathogens may be lurking inside. Having that said, you should always boil any surface water you acquire. Boil your water for at least 3 minutes in order to make sure you kill any harmful agents that may be lurking inside.

Catch Water in Rain Barrels

Besides surface water, in most places you can also easily catch water in a rain barrel. Simply put the barrel out into the open and wait for it to rain. Your rain barrel will steadily capture whatever falls into it. Just be careful before drinking. Because just like any surface water, rain that has fallen from the sky can be contaminated with airborne pollution before it even hits the ground. So be sure to boil any rainwater before drinking it, just like you would for surface water.

<u>*Extract Water from Plants*</u>

Direct water extraction from plants is a little-known survival tactic, but it is highly effective. Plants even during a drought will naturally carry their own store of water. Plants consume h2O just like any other creature, and whatever had been rained upon them in recent months is stored up in their leaves, stems and roots. In order to forcibly extract some of this water all you have to do is squeeze it out of them. This can be achieved through the use of a "transpiration bag". Place a small plastic bag over one of the stems of the plant and tie it tightly in place. With this bag in place, as the plant goes through its daily cycle, it will release its water stores right into the bag. This method does not produce a large amount of water, but in an emergency, it creates just enough to survive.

Collect Water Through Solar Sills

The use of a solar sill is actually a more complex method of water extraction from plants that can bring a higher yield of water. Solar sills work by digging up a small hole, placing a receptacle of some sort at the bottom of it, and then laying out some tarp over the top of the depression. Bury the edges of the tarp under the ground to hold it in place, and then gather up as much fresh vegetation as you can find and toss them into the center of your tarp, just over the water receptacle underneath. Now when the sun strikes the plant material, and causes condensation to form, all of the moisture will drip down off of the plants through the tarp and into your water container below. This is a clever way to collect water a good amount of water.

Carry Extra Water

One of the easiest means of making sure you have water during your trip into the wilderness, is to simply carry an extra supply to begin with. If you can manage it, stuff an entire extra backpack with as many bottles of water as you can find. That way, if you conserve your water consumption, you should be able to last for quite a long time without any new additions of water being needed. Carry extra water, just in case you need it later on.

Drink Recycled Urine

The gross out factor of this option is obvious, but if you are stranded in the middle of some wilderness dessert somewhere with no other possible means of water acquisition in sight. Recycling your own urine may be the only way to stave off death by dehydration. But how is it done?

One of the easiest ways to do it, is through the use of a solar sill. Just create a solar sill as mentioned in the previous section, but instead of placing plants in the center of the sill, you are going to place urine. Yes, that's right, the sill will work as a filter, and as soon as the sun strikes your urine, it will boil away contaminates, while the H2O remaining in the urine drops through the tarp and into the water receptacle. This recycled water should now be separated from contaminants, and safe to drink. It's not always a pretty picture, but its survival!

Chapter 4: Making Campfires and Staying Warm

If you are stuck out in the wilderness when the sun goes down, you will need to find a way to stay warm. In this chapter we will explore how to make adequate campfires and other means of staying warm.

Using Old Fashioned Fire Drills

Fire drills are an ancient standby when it comes to sparking your own fire. The method consists of taking a stick and placing it over a flat wooden board and rubbing the stick between your open palms. As you rapidly roll the stick between your hands, the friction of "drilling" the bottom of the stick into the board will eventually create a spark to light a campfire. It's as simple as that!

Making Sparks with Flint Rock

Flint rocks have been used since prehistoric times. These special little rocks can create a spark simply by striking them together. They are very useful and convenient to have, and work almost anywhere. These flint rocks are even better than fire drills, because they can be used even in the most adverse of weather conditions. Fire drills might not work during a rain storm by flint rocks will. So be sure to bring some with you.

Using Adequate Tinder

The kind of tinder you use will determine what kind of fire that you will have. Soft woods are good for a gentle blaze used for cooking, whereas hardwoods are good for a heartier, longer burning fire used to keep the camp warm. You also need to be sure to arrange your tinder properly in the center of the fire, and make sure that it is adequately stocked at all times.

Establishing a Fire Place

Building a simple stone fire place for your wilderness campfire will help you to better control the flames that you are using to stay warm. Just place a series of stones into a circle, and put your tinder material into the center of it. This stone circle should serve to keep your blazing tinder, and as a consequence—your fire, well within the circular framework of your fire place. This way you don't have to worry too much about your fire getting out of control, and it will stay relatively well maintained. A stone fireplace also serves as a great camp marker. And should you get lost, it will be a great landmark to find your way back again.

Chapter 5: Finding and Preparing Food

It may not have the convenience of a McDonald's drive thru, but some of the best food can be found out in the middle of the wilderness. Here, we will discuss some of the best ways to find and prepare food while you are in the great outdoors.

Berries

In the wilderness you will come across many instances of berries growing naturally in the foliage. Blueberries, blackberries, cranberries, raspberries, and even strawberries can all be found growing quite naturally, in the wilderness. The biggest concern with consuming these berries, is to make sure you don't eat a batch that is poisonous. Most berries you find should be find, but there are a few non-edible varieties that you need to look out for.

One of these are the so-called "ghost berries" that are nearly pure white in appearance. Also, strikingly bright red berries may be of concern as well. Even if you are sure by sight that your berries are safe, you should always administer a taste test before consuming them. This means placing one of the berries on your tongue without eating it, and letting it just sit there for a few moments. If you do not perceive a bad taste, and do not have any other adverse reactions, the berries should be fine to eat.

Mushrooms

You can find these little guys growing at the foot of trees in the forest or growing out on the open ground. Mushrooms are highly nutritious foods, and a great resource to forage. Just be careful not to eat a poisonous mushroom. Most poisonous mushrooms are rather obvious due to bright and elaborate colorings. But if you are not sure whether a mushroom is poisonous or not, you can administer a taste test by tearing off a small piece of the fungus and sticking it on the top of your tongue. If after several minutes you do not have an adverse reaction, the mushroom should be safe for consumption.

Acorns

Acorns are a tasty little morsel found all over the forest floor of wooded environments. Gather as many of these as you can, rinse them off and crack them open. They can be eaten plain, or you can grind them up and use them as a kind of flour. Some have even made pancakes out of acorns. Nothing quite like wilderness acorn flap jacks!

<u>*Dandelions*</u>

You may have notice these yellow little guys popping up out of the ground during the Spring and Summer months. They are quite ubiquitous, and are essentially a weed. But even though they are considered a pest and the bane of landscapers, dandelions are edible and quite nutritious. Just one dandelion is full of important vitamins and minerals. You can eat dandelions raw or you could boil them and eat them in stews and soups. If you are starving in the wilderness, dandelions will provide you with much needed nourishment.

Fishing is an ancient enterprise. People have been casting their lines into the water to bring up their next meal for thousands of years. You too can fish with a traditional fishing line, or you could use a fishing spear. Fishing spears are simply wooden implements that are used to stab into the water until a fish is pierced and brought to the surface. Another method of fishing is to use an inverted water bottle to trap them. In order to do this, simply cut off the end of a water bottle, and invert the mouth inside the bottle. This way, fish can swim into the bottle but by means of suction, are not able to get out. Attach a string to the end of this bottle and throw it down into a stream. Pretty soon you will have plenty of fish to eat.

Chapter 6: Taking Care of Your Health

If your health suffers, everything suffers. Even in the wilderness you need to take care to make good decisions for your physical wellbeing. In this chapter we will focus on both over the counter and natural remedies that will serve you well during your sojourn in the wilderness.

First Aid Kit

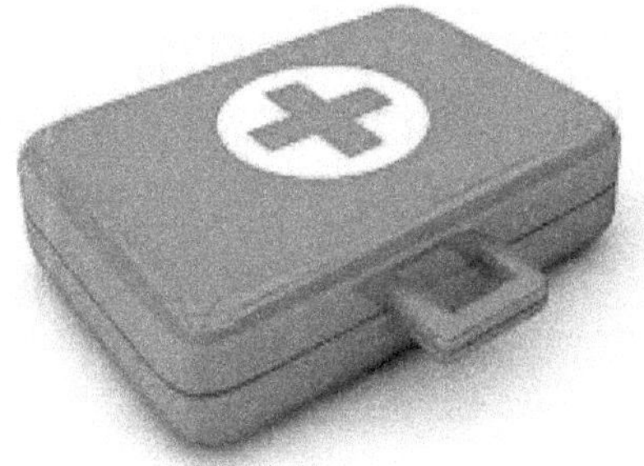

For anyone thinking about trekking into the unknown wilderness, you need to consider taking a First Aid Kit with you. First Aid Kit's should have such health staples, as aspirin, bandages, cold packs, tweezers, thread, and scissors. The thread and scissors may be necessary for example, in order to sew up wounds and create stiches. Bring a First Aid Kit for all of your potential health needs.

<u>*Aloe Vera*</u>

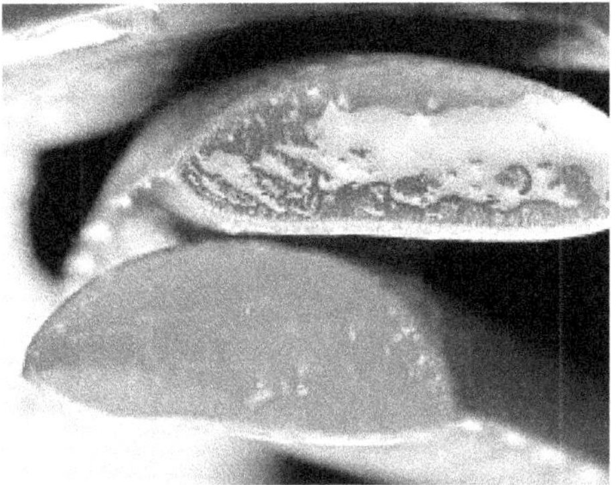

If you have ever been sunburned and rubbed some Aloe Vera gel onto the burn, you know just how soothing this stuff really is. Aloe Vera gel works to rebuild damaged skin tissue, and just a small application can greatly bolster the healing process of skin cells. Along with burns, Aloe Vera is good for treating just about any skin damage, such as cuts, scrapes, and sores. Be sure to pack some Aloe Vera for your journey!

Garlic

Garlic has been used to treat and disinfect wounds since the days of the ancient Greeks. Most today are probably more familiar with Garlic as an additive to food, but Garlic is also a healing herb. Garlic can is a natural antibiotic that kills germs on contact. It also works as a immune boosting agent the instant the aroma of Garlic is inhaled. It is due to the latter that an old folk remedy to ward off sickness was to wear a necklace of garlic. Hollywood later took this remedy and transformed it as a prop to ward off vampires. But even though garlic probably won't ward off Dracula, it will ward off the flu bug!

Burdock Root Salve

This amazing, and all-natural Burdock Root Salve does wonders to relieve the inflammation of arthritis. If you have chronic arthritis, rubbing just a little bit of this salve onto your joints will help to relieve it. But it's not only good for arthritis, burdock root is good for just about any painful ache you may have. I can remember a year ago when I was hiking through the woods and tripped and sprained my ankle. I applied a little bit of this Burdock Root Salve and felt better in no time! Burdock Root Salve packs a punch! Bring it with you for your next foray into the wilderness!

Conclusion: Taking Our Cues from Nature

This book has provided you with 25 hacks essential to your survival in the wilderness. Take note of them, and use them all for your full advantage. But beyond the 25 hacks presented here in this book, the most important hack is your own self confidence. Be self-assured that your sojourn in the great outside will be successful beforehand and it most likely will be. Just take your cues from nature and let your own determination do the rest. Thank you for reading!